Bb

Bela Davis

Abdo
THE ALPHABET
Kids

abdopublishing.com

Published by Abdo Kids, a division of ABDO, PO Box 398166, Minneapolis, Minnesota 55439.
Copyright © 2017 by Abdo Consulting Group, Inc. International copyrights reserved in all countries.
No part of this book may be reproduced in any form without written permission from the publisher.

Printed in the United States of America, North Mankato, Minnesota.

102016
012017

THIS BOOK CONTAINS
RECYCLED MATERIALS

Photo Credits: iStock, Shutterstock

Production Contributors: Teddy Borth, Jennie Forsberg, Grace Hansen

Design Contributors: Christina Doffing, Candice Keimig, Dorothy Toth

Publisher's Cataloging in Publication Data

Names: Davis, Bela, author.

Title: Bb / by Bela Davis.

Description: Minneapolis, Minnesota : Abdo Kids, 2017 | Series: The alphabet |
    Includes bibliographical references and index.

Identifiers: LCCN 2016943881 | ISBN 9781680808780 (lib. bdg.) |
    ISBN 9781680795882 (ebook) | ISBN 9781680796551 (Read-to-me ebook)

Subjects: LCSH: English language--Alphabet--Juvenile literature. | Alphabet
    books--Juvenile literature.

Classification: DDC 421/.1--dc23

LC record available at http://lccn.loc.gov/2016943881

Table of Contents

Bb

Brooke has **b**irthday fun.

Bb

Ben has six **b**alloons.

Bb

Brianna reads a **b**ook.

Bb

Brady **basks** on the **b**each.

Bb

Bailey works with **b**eads.

13

Bb

Bob likes to shoot **b**askets.

Bb

Brittany holds a **b**ase**b**all **b**at.

Bb

Brynn blows on a **dandelion**.

Bb

What does **B**ruce have?

(a **b**unny)

More **Bb** Words

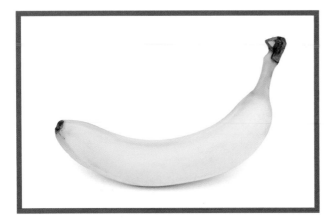
banana

butterfly

blue jay

buttons

Glossary

bask
lie exposed to warmth and light in order to relax.

dandelion
a weed in the daisy family.

Index

abdokids.com

Use this code to log on to abdokids.com and access crafts, games, videos, and more!

Abdo Kids Code:
TBK8780